HISTORY & GEOGRAPHY 708
Political Science

LIFEPAC Test is located in the center of the booklet. Please remove before starting the unit.

Author:
Alpha Omega Staff

Editor:
Alan Christopherson, M.S.

Westover Studios Design Team:
Phillip Pettet, Creative Lead
Teresa Davis, DTP Lead
Nick Castro
Andi Graham
Jerry Wingo

Alpha Omega
PUBLICATIONS

804 N. 2nd Ave. E.
Rock Rapids, IA 51246-1759

Political Science

Introduction

Since the beginning of history, men have lived in organized groups. These groups have ranged in size from a few related families to nations with several million people. Groups of any size, whether they be bands, clans, tribes, or nations, have at least two things in common. All groups have leaders, and each group has rules or laws that specify how its members should act. Usually, these rules are based on the religious and philosophical beliefs of the majority of the group.

The ancient tribes of Israel possessed laws based upon the *Torah*, the first five books of the Old Testament: Genesis, Exodus, Leviticus, Numbers, and Deuteronomy. These laws were carried out by the politico-religious leaders. Modern nations such as the United States possess rules made by the agreement of the citizens and carried out by the various branches of government. The study of the leaders and the laws of various nations, as well as the people who were governed by them, is the focus of political science.

In this LIFEPAC® you will learn why political scientists consider their focus for studying the history of man to be important. You will learn the meaning of terms such as freedom, rights, and human dignity and the part these concepts play in Western civilization. You will also study some of the ideas that important Western political thinkers have written. This LIFEPAC will help you understand more fully some of the foundational ideas of your family, your society, and your country.

Objectives

Read these objectives. The objectives tell you what you will be able to do when you have successfully completed this LIFEPAC. When you have finished this LIFEPAC, you should be able to:

1. Discuss the subject matter of political science.

2. Identify the three general categories of political science.

3. Explain the difference between explanation and description and tell why this difference is important in the study of political science.

4. Discuss the three bases of human knowledge.

5. Outline the goal of political science.

6. Identify the contributions of Jewish civilization to Western political thought.

7. List the contributions of Greek civilization to Western political thought.

8. Identify the contributions of Christianity to Western political thought.

9. List the contributions of some modern political thinkers.

10. Explain the use of models in political science.

11. Construct a model of government based upon current events.

Survey the LIFEPAC. Ask yourself some questions about this study and write your questions here.

1. WHAT POLITICAL SCIENCE IS

Political science is concerned with one aspect of man's culture—the rules and procedures man uses to govern himself. The process of making rules to live by and putting these rules into practice in society is called politics. In the study of politics, political scientists want to know how the individuals in a group are organized to carry out the goals of that group. They ask questions about the power relationships that exist between individuals or sections of a group. Political scientists try to identify who the leaders are and how they obtained their positions and power. Political scientists also examine the process by which decisions are made concerning the allocation of a nation's resources.

Harold Lasswell, a twentieth-century political scientist, defined political science as "the study of who gets what, when and how." Although this definition is very simple, it is a good description of what a political scientist does.

In this section of the LIFEPAC you will learn that political scientists make a distinction between description (telling what you have seen) and explanation (telling how you think what you have seen works). You will learn that this distinction is based upon the ways in which we see the world and upon the ways we collect facts to make up knowledge. We use this knowledge in describing and explaining what we see.

SECTION OBJECTIVES

Review these objectives. When you have completed this section, you should be able to:

1. Discuss the subject matter of political science.

2. Identify the three general categories of political science.

3. Explain the difference between explanation and description and tell why this distinction is important in the study of political science.

4. Discuss the three bases of human knowledge.

5. Outline the goal of political science.

VOCABULARY

Study these words to enhance your learning success in this section.

allocation (al' u kā shun). Allotment or distribution, especially by a government.

empiricism (em pir' u siz um). The idea that knowledge is based upon the physical senses.

epistemology (i pis' tu mol' u jē). The study of how we know what we know.

fideism (fī' dē iz um). The idea that knowledge is based upon faith.

politics (pol' u tiks). The process of governing; the making of rules for a group or nation.

rationalism (rash' u nu liz um). The idea that knowledge is based upon logical human thought.

theorist (thē' ur ist). A thinker.

Note: *All vocabulary words in this LIFEPAC appear in* boldface *print the first time they are used. If you are not sure of the meaning when you are reading, study the definitions given.*

Pronunciation Key: hat, āge, cãre, fär; let, ēqual, tėrm; it, īce; hot, ōpen, ôrder; oil; out; cup, pu̇t, rüle; child; long; thin; /ŦH/ for then; /zh/ for measure; /u/ or /ə/ represents /a/ in about, /e/ in taken, /i/ in pencil, /o/ in lemon, and /u/ in circus.

AREAS OF POLITICAL SCIENCE

Even though political science is limited to the study of the political aspects of man's culture, this area for study is very wide. Because of the great amount of political knowledge available, most political scientists study only small special areas. Like the historian who studies only the history of England or the sociologist who specializes in the behavior of disadvantaged groups, the modern political scientist chooses an area small enough for him to study in depth. Although these areas of specialized study are many, they can be grouped for our purposes into three main categories: political theory, comparative government, and epistemology. All of these categories overlap so much that a political scientist must have at least some knowledge in each of them. His interests cannot be so specialized that he excludes associated areas of politics from his studies.

Political theory. The first of these general categories, political theory, has as a central concern the philosophical basis of man's systems of government. A political theorist may ask basic questions about how governments are formed and where the leaders in a government obtain their power. He could be told that a ruler's power is a grant from God, like the anointing of David by Samuel, or that the power of the leader is part of a contract made among the citizens of a nation. A political thinker or theorist may also seek to know about political alternatives within a group. He could ask what would happen if the people of a group no longer accepted the form of government under which they have been living.

Political theory is concerned with how man forms and views his governments. Political theory also includes the study of the history of man's thoughts about the various governments that have existed and the relationship of the rules of a government to the rights of an individual under that government. Much of the way in which modern nations are governed is based on the thoughts of political thinkers who lived

as long ago as two thousand years. Because these ideas are still accepted and are passed from one theorist to another so often, they are generally referred to as the tradition of Western political thought.

Comparative government. Comparative government is the study of the ways in which governments work. Comparative government includes the descriptions of the operations within nations, the process of politics in these nations, and the political institutions that help organize a nation. These studies have become so detailed that some political scientists refer to comparative government as the study of the "machinery of government."

Some specific studies in comparative government include political parties and elections, various governments of the world (of which United States government is one such study), and international relations, the study of how nations interact with each other. A political scientist interested in comparative government could also study the political behaviors or cultures of groups within a nation. He may want to discover where these citizens get their political beliefs and why they act as they do toward their government. A final area of study within comparative government is public administration. Public administration is the method of actually operating government and public institutions.

Complete the vocabulary crossword.

1.1 **ACROSS**

1. a thinker
2. the idea that knowledge is based on logical human thought
3. allotment or distribution, especially by a government
4. the idea that knowledge is based upon the physical senses

DOWN

5. the process of governing; the making of rules for a group or nation
6. the idea that knowledge is based on faith
7. the study of how we know what we know

Complete these statements.

1.2 Two things that all organized groups have in common are a. _____ and

b. _____ .

1.3 The process of man governing of himself is called _____ .

1.4 The rules of a group are based upon the a. _____ or

b. _____ beliefs of the majority of that group.

1.5 Two of the general categories of political science are a. _____

and b. _____ .

1.6 International relations is the study of how _____ interact with each other.

Epistemology. The final category of study in political science is called epistemology. This impressive word, *epistemology*, means *how we know what we know.* All political scientists are concerned with epistemology in their studies, regardless of their specialized interests. Understanding knowledge is important to political science because few things are discussed as much, and with as much emotion, and have as many possible interpretations as politics.

People have always had a concern for the way in which their governments have been operated. Many people have made statements like "this is the very best form of government," or "the Republican Party is the party of the rich." Political scientists need to know the nature of the evidence that supports these types of statements. Therefore, the political scientist not only asks questions about how nations and the people in them behave, but he also seeks to understand the basis for the political opinions of the people. He is concerned about the type of evidence to which people refer in answer to his questions about their political behavior.

 Complete these statements.

1.7 Political scientists are concerned with the _____ of nations and people.

1.8 Political scientists seek to understand the basis for the political _____ of the people.

1.9 _____ is the study of how we know what we know.

1.10 If a political scientist is told, "Democrats are wealthy," he would look for _____ that supports that statement.

WAYS OF KNOWING

Between the time that you were born and now, you have collected many facts about how the world in which you live works. You have learned about how the people around you behave and what to expect from the world around you from day to day. All of the facts that you know, when added together, make up the body of knowledge you use to make decisions about how to conduct your life. Not all of the facts that you know come from the same source, and not all of them have the same value to you as far as being useful, correct, or even believable.

Discovering how people know what they know is one of the first steps in understanding the methods that political scientists use in studying governments. Scholars refer to three general ways in which people can know things: empiricism, rationalism, and fideism.

Empiricism. The way of knowing that relies on our physical senses is called empiricism. We continually experience our world through our senses. Through sight, touch, and smell children first learn what a flower is. Through sight and sound they also learn what an airplane is and what it does. By seeing, touching, or smelling many flowers, a child will learn a whole class of things that fit the word *flower*. In the same way, a child learns about *airplane* by seeing and hearing many airplanes. Although a single flower or airplane may be different from any other the child has experienced, he will know empirically to what class they belong.

Our sense experiences provide us with most of the knowledge we use in daily life. However, empirical knowledge is not always reliable. We can be tricked by our senses into believing what is not really so. Look at the two lines A and B to the right, without measuring them decide which of them is longer.

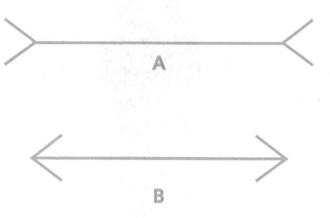

Both of these lines are the same length. However, without using a ruler to extend your empirical knowledge, your sense of sight will probably not provide an accurate measurement.

Now look at the first box and decide which way the front (the side toward you) faces. Does it have the corners ABCD toward you?

Perhaps the second box is facing toward you with the corners EFGH in front.

As you can see, reality is not always as it seems to be. The world has many mirages, like those you see on hot pavement in the summer. This mirage consists in seeing that the road at a distance is full of water. Empirically, you cannot tell that the mirage is being caused by rising heat.

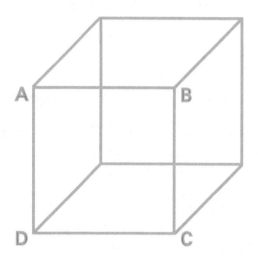

Empirical knowledge is sometimes misleading. In the exercise with the sketched box, the position of the observer or the position of the object being observed can affect what we sense. Man's position on the face of the earth led him to believe for thousands of years that the sun really did "rise" in the east and "set" in the west as it circled the earth.

The illustrations at the top of the next page show two different views of the same thing. As you can see, large insects are crawling up each side of the trunk. However, if you were to change your position and view the other side of the tree, you would find that these "insects" are the claws of a bear climbing the tree.

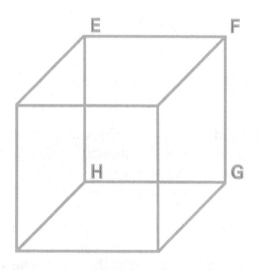

Empirical knowledge may be defended on the grounds that we would not be misled if we had all of the facts. However, empirical knowledge alone is not sufficient to allow people to study thoroughly or to function adequately in the world.

Rationalism. A second source of knowledge is logical thinking, or rationalism. Rationalism emphasizes the ideas of the mind more than the knowledge that we gain by physical senses. Because of rational thought, we accept things because they seem to fit what we already know. Rational knowledge is very much like completing a jigsaw puzzle—the last few pieces fit easily into the established picture.

Look at the following series of letters and decide what they stand for. Fill in the final two letters in this series.

$a \times a = a$	$b \times a = b$	$c \times a = c$
$a \times b = b$	$b \times b = d$	$c \times b = \underline{\quad}$
$a \times c = c$	$b \times c = f$	$c \times c = \underline{\quad}$

You probably discovered that these letters are the beginning of the multiplication tables, with letters standing for numbers— $a = 1$, $b = 2$, $c = 3$ and so on. The pattern that was created was reasonable enough that you probably did not need to know the "answers" to the column with the blanks in it. You accepted your conclusions about the letters and what they meant because the letters fit a pattern that you knew.

Look at the following series of letters and fill in the one that is missing:

S	M	T	W	_	F	S

The missing letter is T. You probably recognized these letters as being the first letters of the days of the week.

S	M	T	W	T	F	S
u	o	u	e	h	r	a
n	n	e	d	u	i	t
d	d	s	n	r	d	u
a	a	d	e	s	a	r
y	y	a	s	d	y	d
		y	d	a		a
			a	y		y
			y			

The answer to this puzzle was not based on empirical knowledge. You used your own sense of sight to the extent that your eyes read the letters. The answer itself was based on rational or logical patterns of thought.

An example of how rationalism is used to understand the world around us can be seen in the question of whether the earth moves around the sun or the sun moves around the earth. If the question is answered only on the basis of empirical knowledge, then we would know that the sun revolves around the earth. However, this answer is not based on a thorough empirical experience. This question should not have been answered empirically until the first astronaut went into space and observed how the earth moved in relationship to the sun. The question was answered rationally in 1543, more than 400 years before the first man left the face of the earth to go into space. Nicolaus Copernicus described the movements of the planets in relation to the sun long before man could fly in airplanes or even move about in automobiles. Through the use of mathematics (a type of rationalism) and reasoning, Copernicus said that the sun is the center of the solar system and that the planets moved around it.

If used by itself, rational knowledge can lead us to believe things that are really not true, just as empirical thought can.

Consider this word problem:

> Since 1865, the governments of Mexico and the United States have had an agreement called the *Dead and Misplaced Persons Treaty*. This agreement says that if a natural disaster occurs near the border between the United States and Mexico, the bodies of the victims of the disaster will be buried in the country in which the disaster took place. Pretend that you are the American ambassador to Mexico and you are told that a plane has crashed exactly on the border of the two countries. The choice is yours. Where would you bury the survivors?

If you answered either Mexico or the United States, you would be in error. The problem is a trick, containing incomplete, conflicting, and untrue information. Therefore, any attempt to answer the question based on what was given to you in the problem would have been in error. If either the problem is stated wrongly or decisions are based on incomplete facts about the problem, the answer will be in error. Rationalism by itself is not a sufficient base for knowledge. All our knowledge will result in an incomplete view of the world.

 Write true or false.

1.11 _____ The three ways in which people can know things are empiricism, rationalism, and fideism.

1.12 _____ Empiricism relies on our physical senses to tell us things we know.

1.13 _____ The use of our senses forms the basis for little of the knowledge we most often use.

1.14 _____ Reality is always what it seems to be.

1.15 _____ A mirage is a true image that we can use.

1.16 _____ Empirical knowledge alone is not enough to allow people to function adequately in the world.

Complete these statements.

1.17 Rationalism emphasizes the idea of the _____ more than the knowledge we gain from our physical senses.

1.18 The movements of the earth were described by _____ .

1.19 Through the use of a. _____ and b. _____ , Copernicus said that the sun was the c. _____ of the solar system with the planets moving around it.

1.20 Rationalism is not a sufficient base for _____ .

Complete this activity.

1.21 Write a rational puzzle similar to the letter puzzles in the text. When you have finished writing your puzzle, have one of your classmates work it.

HELPER CHECK _____ _____
                        initials   date

Fideism. Fideism comes from the Latin word meaning *faith* and refers to a way of knowing. This method of knowing is based on our inner feelings. We can know things simply through an act of faith. The belief in a Supreme Being is not based on empirical knowledge because we have never seen God with our physical senses. This belief is also not based on rationalism. Although many people have attempted to prove the existence or nonexistence of God through rational means, the question of God's existence cannot be settled by totally rational means. One simply has faith that God exists. As the Bible says (Hebrews 11:6), "...he that cometh to God must believe that he is...."

Fideism also extends to our emotions, knowing how we feel. For example, we do not need our eyes or our logical thoughts to tell us that we feel love. Our love for others is expressed through what we do, but it is known by how we feel.

Using fideism as the only base for our knowledge about earthly things could be very harmful. A person who has faith in someone and follows his orders could be committing a wrongful act. The appropriateness of an action done at the request of a person will be related to the integrity of that person. A person of high integrity will direct others to do righteous acts; likewise, one of low integrity will lead others to sin.

Also, knowledge based completely on faith can be misleading if the source of the knowledge is false. For example, those who attempt to conduct their lives by reading the horoscope in the daily newspaper are following a false guide.

On the other hand, those who conduct their lives by the Scriptures have a sure guide for life (Psalm 119:105): "Thy word is a lamp unto my feet and a light unto my path." Occasionally, we use each of the three ways of knowing separately; but, more commonly, we use them in combination. Our rational thoughts, our faith, and our senses work together in gaining knowledge.

If you were visiting a foreign country where all of the traffic lights were white and flashed different symbols instead of the colors red, yellow, and green, you may have a difficult time deciding when to cross the street safely.

If you saw the cars stop at the intersection every time the light marked x was on, you could conclude after watching long enough, that x always means stop. In the same manner, if the cars drove through the intersection when the + light was on, the + would evidently mean go. Your conclusion about what these two traffic signals mean is based on observation of the cars—empirical knowledge. The conclusion that the cars *always* stop on x and *always* go on + is rational knowledge because you have decided that the signals form a pattern which should continue as long as cars, stop lights, and laws continue in that country.

If a very good friend told you that ✳ meant that the cars were supposed to slow down and you believed him, you would then have knowledge based on faith.

The methods of gaining knowledge—empiricism, rationalism, and fideism—have been the basis of political science throughout history. All of these ways of knowing have been used by political scientists to explain behavior in the world of governments and to *predict* what will happen in the future. The goal of political science is twofold: to explain and to predict.

In the next section of this LIFEPAC, you will learn how political philosophers have used each of these methods of gaining knowledge to explain or to predict political events.

Complete these activities.

The following statements are based upon empirical knowledge, rational knowledge, or faith. Put *E* for empirical, *R* for rational, or *F* for faith. Some of the statements are based on more than one type of knowledge.

1.22 _____ When the crosswalk guard says I can cross the street, the cars will stop for me.

1.23 _____ Plants need water to live.

1.24 _____ If two times two is four, then two times three is six.

1.25 _____ If you throw a rock up into the air, it will come down.

1.26 _____ "My grandfather told me that the Democrats will put the country into debt, and I believe him."

1.27 _____ The earth is round.

1.28 _____ My parents will keep me safe.

1.29 _____ Birds fly south because the weather is too cold for them in the north.

1.30 _____ If I study hard enough, then I should get an A.

Review the material in this section in preparation for the Self Test. The Self Test will check your mastery of this particular section. The items missed on this Self Test will indicate specific areas where restudy is needed for mastery.

SELF TEST 1

Complete these statements (each answer, 3 points).

1.01 All groups have two things in common: a. _____ and b. _____ .

1.02 The rules of groups are based upon the a. _____ and b. _____ beliefs of the majority of the groups.

1.03 Political science is the study of the a. _____ , b. _____ , and people who make up a nation.

1.04 The process of governing and making rules to live by is called _____ .

1.05 Knowledge based on the senses is called _____ knowledge.

1.06 According to Harold Lasswell, _____ science is "the study of who gets what, when and how."

Write the letter of the correct answer on the line (each answer, 2 points).

1.07 The goal of political science is _____ .
   a. description and explanation
   c. rational and empirical
   b. not usually stated
   d. explanation and prediction

1.08 "The sky is blue" is a(n) _____ statement.
   a. rational
   b. empirical
   c. faith
   d. nonsense

1.09 "The Lord is my shepherd" is a statement based upon _____ .
   a. senses
   b. faith
   c. thought
   d. the Old Testament

1.010 The study of how government and public institutions are operated is the study of _____ .
   a. political theory
   c. public administration
   b. empiricism
   d. election processes

1.011 A political theorist may ask questions about how _____ .
   a. thoughts are formed
   c. theories are formed
   b. classes are formed
   d. governments are formed

1.012 "God created the heavens and the earth" is a statement of _____ .
   a. source knowledge
   c. empirical knowledge
   b. faith knowledge
   d. rational knowledge

1.013 Epistemology is the study of _____ .
   a. political science
   b. philosophy
   c. how we know
   d. rationalism

1.014 Which of the following is not included in comparative government? _____ .
   a. social customs
   c. governments of the world
   b. political institutions
   d. political beliefs

1.015 "After hours of thought, I have decided that green cows could exist" is a statement of _____ .
   a. faith knowledge
   c. rational knowledge
   b. empirical knowledge
   d. sense knowledge

Write true or false (each answer, 1 point).

1.016 _____ Political science is the study of religious beliefs in a nation.

1.017 _____ Empirical knowledge is based on the senses.

1.018 _____ Rational knowledge is based on faith and not on logical thought.

1.019 _____ Epistemology is the study of how we know what we know.

1.020 _____ Rationalism is accepting facts as knowledge because they fit like the pieces of a jig-saw puzzle.

1.021 _____ We cannot be misled by relying on any one of the means of knowledge.

1.022 _____ Political scientists are not interested in the kind of knowledge on which the answers to questions are based.

1.023 _____ Copernicus said that the sun was the center of the solar system.

1.024 _____ The use of our senses forms the basis for little of the knowledge we most often use.

Complete these statements (each answer, 3 points).

1.025 Knowledge based upon logical thought or patterns is called _____ .

1.026 _____ relies on our physical senses to tell us things we know.

1.027 Fideism comes from the Latin root word meaning _____ .

50	
63	

SCORE _____   TEACHER _____ _____
                                                initials   date

2. ROOTS OF WESTERN POLITICAL THOUGHT

Political science is the oldest of all the social sciences. From the time of the first written records, people have been making rules, selecting leaders, and discussing the ways of governing men. Records of laws that date from 2600 BC have been found from the ancient kingdoms of China. Reports of discussions of laws and the conflicts over the method of government a nation should use are nearly as old in the Western world. For example, the Bible reports how the government of Israel changed from that of a single leader, like they followed in their wanderings in the wilderness, to a form of government using appointed judges to settle all of the tribal disputes (Deuteronomy 16:18). When the system of judges became too corrupt through the misuse of power, the elders of Israel told Samuel (1 Samuel 8:18 and 19): "...we will have a king over us; that we also may be like all the nations."

In this section of the LIFEPAC, you will study the three roots of Western political thought: Jewish civilization, Greek civilization, and Christianity. You will learn what each of these roots of thought has contributed to the way in which governments are run, the way in which people are treated under the rules or laws of a government, and the way in which a person's relationship with his government is perceived.

SECTION OBJECTIVES

Review these objectives. When you have completed this section, you should be able to:

6. Identify the contributions of Jewish civilization to Western political thought.

7. List the contributions of Greek civilization to Western political thought.

8. Identify the contributions of Christianity to Western political thought.

VOCABULARY

Study these words to enhance your learning success in this section.

anarchy (an' ur kē). A state of society without government or laws.

aristocracy (ar' u stok' ru sē). A class of hereditary nobility.

cyclical (sī' klu kul). Revolving or recurring in cycles.

franchise (fran' chīz). The right to vote or participate in government.

hierarchy (hī' u rär kē). Any system of things or people in graded order.

Mosaic Code (Mō zā' ik kō d). The Law of Moses.

oligarchy (ol' u gär kē). A form of government where the power is held by a few persons.

republic (ri pub' lik). A form of government where the citizens vote for representatives to direct the state.

THE CONTRIBUTIONS OF JEWISH CIVILIZATION

Almost fourteen hundred years before the birth of Christ, a large group of people fled from the kingdom of Egypt. According to Exodus 12:37, more than six hundred thousand people left the land of Egypt where they had lived for 430 years. These people left with all of their possessions and walked into one of the most barren and lifeless deserts in the world. The physical conditions under which these people lived for the next forty years must have been almost unbearable and extremely dangerous. The social condition in which the Hebrews found themselves was just as dangerous to their continued existence as a people as was the lack of water and food. For as long as any of this group of wanderers could remember, they had been subjects of the Egyptian government. They had lived under Egyptian laws, worked for the increase of the power of Egypt, and had been governed by an Egyptian ruler, the Pharaoh.

The Hebrews left behind not only the homes where they and their parents, grandparents, and great-grandparents had lived but also the rules by which their society had been governed for more than four hundred years. The Exodus would be comparable to the people of an

average-sized city in the United States packing up all the belongings they could carry and walking away. They would leave behind the mayors, city councilmen, policemen, congressmen, and others who made the rules and laws under which they lived, as well as leaving the laws themselves. If this happened today, we would expect many disputes and arguments over all of the loose property that was being carried around. We also would find enough dishonest persons to cause problems within the group.

A term that could be applied to the type of situation where no laws or leadership exists is **anarchy**. Occasionally, the Hebrews experienced times of anarchy where each man did that which was right in his own eyes. Nevertheless, after leaving Egypt, the Hebrews were governed by the judgments of Moses and then by God's Law, the Ten Commandments.

Moses. Moses, the leader of the Hebrews, tried to correct the instability of the people by sitting in judgment over all the disputes

that arose. Moses found the situation to be so confusing and so overwhelming that he could not handle it by himself without becoming worn out and losing the respect of the people (Exodus 18:13–26). To ease his own burden and still keep disputes under control, Moses constructed a loose political organization. He appointed men whom he trusted to make the decisions and judgments that had formerly been handled by the Egyptian system of rules. These men were placed in a **hierarchy**. Each of those at the lowest level was in charge of ten people. The next level of leaders, where more difficult decisions were made, was in charge of five of these groups of ten. The next level of leaders was in charge of a hundred and the last level contained the leaders of groups of one thousand. In this way only the most important decisions and judgments would be made by Moses. All of the more trivial matters, such as who owned what goat, would be decided at the lower levels of this desert government.

After the Hebrews had been in the wilderness for three months, God and Moses spoke of a code of laws under which this new nation of people would live.

 Complete the vocabulary crossword.

2.1 ACROSS

1. a state of society without government or laws
2. a form of government where the power is held by a few persons
3. the Law of Moses

DOWN

1. a class of hereditary nobility
2. a form of government where the citizens vote for representatives to direct the state
3. any system of things or people in graded order
4. the right to vote or participate in government
5. revolving or recurring in cycles

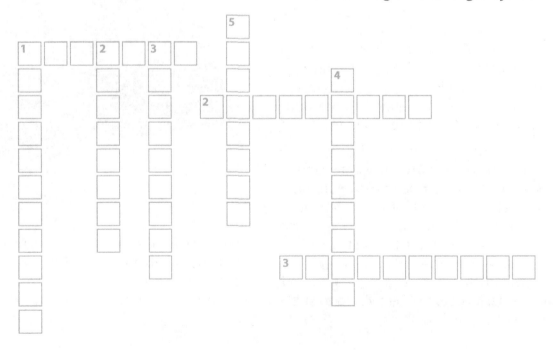

Complete these statements.

2.2 More than a. _____ people left Egypt under the leadership of b. _____ .

2.3 The Egyptian ruler was also known as the _____ .

2.4 The state where a group of people who are without laws or leadership is called _____ .

2.5 The system where things or people are in graded order is called a _____ .

 Read Exodus 21 and 22; Leviticus 6 and 24; and Deuteronomy 17.

The Law. The Commandments that Moses brought down from Mount Sinai are the basis of Jewish law. However, other codes of law existed before the Mosaic Code. Hammurabi, a Babylonian king, had his code of laws written around 2100 BC The importance of the Mosaic Code in Western political thought is seen in three areas: man's relationship with his leaders, man's relationship to the nation or state, and man's relationship with his fellow man.

Moses stated that the Law he had given to the Hebrews has one source, the living God. The law would no longer be based upon the word of whatever Pharaoh or king ruled, but upon the word of God. Because the Law came from God, the leaders were bound to obey the laws just as were the ordinary citizens. The Law would, therefore, be unchanging and unchangeable; it could not be twisted to suit the purposes of the leaders.

The Law was also important because it marked the first time that any set of moral laws was considered valid for all men. (The ceremonial laws are considered to be restricted to Israel.)

Since only one God made all people, this one set of moral rules should apply to all. Before this time, laws and rules were only made for the protection of the members of a certain group or nation. For instance, if the Babylonians had a law that said "Thou shall not kill" it meant "Thou shalt not kill Babylonians." In fact, most primitive people did not (and in some societies still do not) believe that others who are not of their tribe are human. The translation of the names of many primitive groups shows the difference between who is human and who is not. Consider the American Indian group from the Southwest, the Apache. These native Americans call themselves *dene'*, which means "the people." Any individual who was not *dene'* was not properly human; the Apache would treat him differently from the way they would treat a

fellow *dene'*. When compared to the restrictive ideas of some groups, the moral Law of Moses bound all men into a brotherhood. This brotherhood was one of responsibility, not salvation (read Romans 2:11–15).

The third area of importance of the Jewish Law was the absence of any tie to a particular governmental structure or geographical location. The Jewish Law had the form of a covenant with God. These moral laws would be binding on people even without the leadership of a king or the enforcement of the state. In whatever part of the world, or under whatever type of governmental structure a person lived, these laws were the same. Even in a state of anarchy, the laws would remain active and binding.

 Match the following items. You may use your Bible.

2.6	_____ witnesses for the prosecution	a.	Exodus 21:46
2.7	_____ one law for all people	b.	Exodus 21:33 and 34; 22:5; 22:14
2.8	_____ interest rates for the poor	c.	Numbers 35:30
2.9	_____ arson	d.	Deuteronomy 17: 8 and 9
2.10	_____ destruction of other people's property	e.	Exodus 21:2–6
2.11	_____ settling difficult disputes	f.	Leviticus 6:2–5
2.12	_____ how to treat strangers	g.	Exodus 22:9
2.13	_____ determining ownership of property	h.	Exodus 22:6
2.14	_____ concealing someone's property	i.	Leviticus 24:22
		j.	Exodus 22:25
		k.	Exodus 22:21

Answer these questions.

2.15 What are the three contributions of Jewish civilization to Western political thought?

a. _____

_____

b. _____

_____

c. _____

_____

2.16 In which areas is the influence of the Mosaic Code seen in Western political thought?

a. _____

b. _____

c. _____

2.17 Who authored the earliest known written code of laws? _____

2.18 Who is the source of the Jewish Law? _____

THE CONTRIBUTIONS OF THE GREEK CIVILIZATION

At about the same time that Moses and the Jews were wandering in the Sinai desert, a group of barbarian invaders, the Greeks, were conquering a more advanced group of people in the south of the Grecian peninsula. In 1400 BC the Greeks were tribes of warriors living in small bands under the rule of tribal kings. In less than one hundred years the bands of invaders had conquered all of Greece and had set up kingdoms based on their tribal groupings. These small kingdoms, called city-states, consisted of a central fortified city surrounded by smaller villages and agricultural lands.

By 500 BC the Greeks had written constitutions for each of their city-states, which specified the laws of how the city-states, or polis, should be governed. These constitutions also included rules of citizenship, telling who was considered a member of the polis and what the citizen's duties to the state were. Each of the city-states was still ruled by a king At that time, however, the king's power had been greatly eroded. He was usually required by the constitution to take into account the wishes of the most influential warriors and the most prominent citizens. The rule of kings had almost totally vanished in the

Peloponnesian peninsula, and rulership was taken over by the councils that had formerly only advised the king. This new form of government, the rule by a few, is called an oligarchy. These governments by oligarchy became so intolerable that they were soon replaced by several different forms of government in the city-states. The most important of these new forms of government appeared in the most famous of the city-states, Athens.

The democracy of Athens. The constitution of Athens specified the most open form of government that had existed to that time. The constitution allowed every adult male citizen the opportunity to take part in government. In fact, the constitution demanded that a citizen take part since his duty was to help the state in all things—including government.

To keep the power of the state out of the hands of only one person or a few people, leaders were elected for a fixed period of time by all the male citizens. Disputes between citizens were decided by a court that had as many as 6,000 elected jurors on hand. Any one court could have as many as 100 jurors hearing a case at one time.

In spite of the fact that Athens allowed such wide participation in the affairs of state, no feeling for individual rights existed. The Greeks of Athens stressed only the duties of the individual to the state, and not the duty of the state to the individual.

In 1,000 years Athens had come from the rule of one warrior king with absolute power to a system of government which stressed that the individual had a duty to participate in politics. Because of the almost countless rulers and varied forms of government that had been tried in Athens, many Athenians were deeply interested in politics and the philosophy of government. Two Athenians who were most important to the study of Western political thought were Plato (427-347 BC) and his student, Aristotle (384-322 BC).

Plato. Plato was a teacher of philosophy, which means that he taught "thinking." Born of an aristocratic family, Plato spent his life traveling, writing, and, later, teaching in a school he founded in Athens called the *Academy*. Of the books he wrote, the most famous is *The Republic*. This book, in which he attempted to describe the ideal form of government, has been called the first political science book in history. The form of government that Plato described is not considered to be important. The important contribution that Plato made was his attitude of asking questions about how men and their nations should behave. Because of Plato's influence, men could observe and prescribe a logical system of government. For the very first time in Western civilization, government was perceived to be coming from the mind of man and not just appearing on its own like the growing grass.

Aristotle. Aristotle, Plato's most famous student, was the son of a doctor in the court of King Philip of Macedon. After studying at Plato's *Academy* for almost twenty years, Aristotle founded his own school in Athens called the *Lyceum*. Aristotle was interested in every subject of the ancient world. He wrote books on biology, logic, literature, political theory, and ethics. Plato was primarily concerned with how things should be in the ideal state; however,

| Aristotle

Aristotle was interested in how things were in reality. His most famous writing on the subject of government was called *The Politics*. In this book Aristotle classified the many kinds of states into three classes: rule by one, rule by a few, and rule by many. This classification has remained basically unchanged in political science from the time of Aristotle.

Aristotle was also influential in his conception of the *rule of law* rather than the *rule of men*. His argument stated that, whatever the form of government, whether rule by one, many, or a few, government could be either good or bad. According to Aristotle, the major factor in making government good was not changing the form of the government but applying a system of laws to all citizens equally.

Greek civilization, especially that of Athens is an important part of the tradition of Western political thought. In general, the democracy of Athens was the original model for our present-day democratic systems of government. Even though the Athenians allowed citizenship and participation in the rule of the city-state only to adult males, this **franchise** was less than 10 percent of the three hundred thousand people living in Athens.

The Athenian democracy showed that the ordinary person was capable of taking part in making the rules which governed the city and in selection of the leaders who would enforce the rules and protect the state.

Plato, influenced by the political experiments of his city-state, gave us the first idea that men could take part in the creation of a nation. Through logical, systematic thought, or rationalism, men could correct the evils of government rather than allow good government to arise by chance.

Plato's student, Aristotle, offered us the first political classification system and stressed that the rule of good laws, rather than the rule of good men, makes good government.

In all of their thinking about government, the Greeks never questioned the belief that the purpose of the citizen was to serve the state. Also, they never asked whether the state had any obligation to protect the rights of the individual citizen. The idea that the individual might have rights and duties more important than serving the state came only with the growth of Christianity.

 Write true or false.

2.19 _____ Aristotle wrote a famous book on politics called *The Republic*.

2.20 _____ The Greeks believed that the purpose of the state was to serve the citizen.

2.21 _____ Aristotle stressed the idea of rule by law.

2.22 _____ *Oligarchy* means the *rule by many*.

2.23 _____ Athens, under democracy, had the most open form of government to that time.

2.24 _____ Plato, a student of Aristotle, wrote of his scheme of government in a book called *The Politics*.

Complete this activity.

2.25 Choose one of the places or persons from the following list and write a one-page report. If you choose a place, tell where it was located, mention some of its important rulers or citizens, and classify its governmental system according to the threefold classification of Aristotle. If you choose a person, tell when the person lived, why he was famous, and what sort of government he lived under according to Aristotle's classification system. (rule by one, rule by few, rule by many).

Chaldea	Nebuchadnezzar II	Knossus	Thebes
Sumer	Darius I	Troy	Pericles
Akkad	Hammurabi	Homer (Iliad)	Solon
Assyria	Carthage	Sparta	Xerxes
Ptolemy	Seleucia	Euclid	Socrates
Sargon	Crete (Minos)	Macedonia	Archimedes

TEACHER CHECK _____ _____
                            initials   date

THE CONTRIBUTIONS OF CHRISTIANITY

The third root of Western political thought is Christianity. The major Christian political thinkers that will be considered came much later in history (after AD 1000) than the Jews or the Greeks that you have studied. However, Christian political thought shares a fundamental similarity with the other two bases of Western political thought: no system of thought, or philosophy, occurs in a vacuum. Before you examine the great thinkers Augustine and Thomas Aquinas, you must first examine the environment and background against which they reacted. A brief examination of the history of the Roman Empire, the birthplace of Christianity, will acquaint you with that environment and background.

Rome. In 509 BC, a tribe of farming people— the Romans—from the peninsula of Italy overthrew the rule of an Etruscan king named Tarquin the Proud. The Romans were influenced culturally by the Greeks who had established colonies in Southern Italy (which were later conquered by the expanding Roman empire). However, their two forms of government differed greatly. The Greeks would meet in a council of all citizens with each citizen having one vote. Roman citizens, however, elected representatives who would vote on the affairs of state for all of the people. This form of government is known as a **republic**.

The Roman Republic lasted in various forms until 27 BC when the first emperor, Augustus Caesar, was crowned. During the almost five hundred years of the Roman Republic, various Roman rulers and their armies had conquered all the world around the Mediterranean Sea. The world into which Christ was born was a Roman world, and the laws under which He was crucified were approved by the Roman senate.

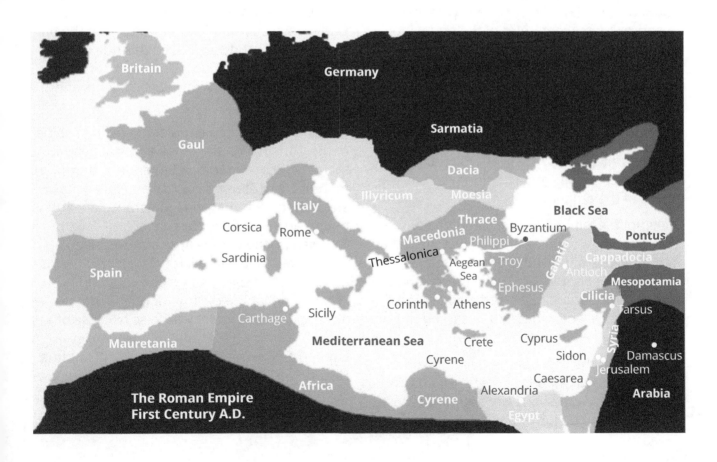

The Roman Empire
First Century A.D.

Write true or false.

2.26 _____ In 509 BC the Roman people defeated Tarquin the Proud.

2.27 _____ Rome was not influenced by the culture of the Greeks.

2.28 _____ The Greeks established colonies in Italy that were later overthrown by the Romans.

2.29 _____ The Greeks met in a council of only some male citizens.

2.30 _____ The Romans had their people elect representatives who voted on the affairs of the state.

2.31 _____ In 27 AD Augustus Caesar became the first Roman emperor.

2.32 _____ A republic is a form of representative government.

Augustine of Hippo. Augustine was a convert to Christianity who later became the bishop of the North African city of Hippo. Little is known of his life, except that he was from a rich and noble family. The Roman Empire at the time of Augustine was in upheaval. To the people of that time, including the Christians who made up approximately one-third of the population of the empire, the world must have seemed as if it were coming to an end. The laws and government of the Roman Empire were about to collapse, after having decided the fate of the Mediterranean world for almost one thousand years. Emperors of this time were selected by Roman armies or by whatever group of powerful men could pay enough money to buy the throne of the emperor.

The empire itself had been divided into two empires with two rulers, and the people in the outer portions of the empire were asserting their right of self-rule. In 410 AD the Visigoths from the "barbarian" lands at the edge of the Roman Empire entered Italy and sacked the city of Rome, the center of the empire.

This attack at the heart of the civilized world caused great fear among some Christians of that age. These Christians were afraid because Christianity had begun and had spread within the threatened Roman Empire. Even though the Roman government had persecuted the Christians for about two hundred fifty years, Rome later gave protection to Christianity and accepted it as the religion of the empire. The identification of Christianity with the Roman state had become very close. If Rome fell, could Christianity also end in the invasions of the barbarians? Augustine answered this question in this book, *The City of God*. This work concerned the relationship of earthly governments and laws with the law of God.

Augustine attempted to quiet the fears of some of the Christians in the empire by stating that the survival of the Roman Empire did not really matter. He wrote that the rise and fall of ideas and nations was only the appearance of earthly things, and all that mattered were the laws of God behind the earthly appearances. Augustine argued that since history is not **cyclical** (as the Greeks believed), it must be continuous. He argued that the cyclical thinking about the development of history was false because of an event that was unique, one that would never happen again. This event was the birth of Christ. History is a line of man's development from Creation to Judgment and Augustine said that along that line extend two communities, or cities.

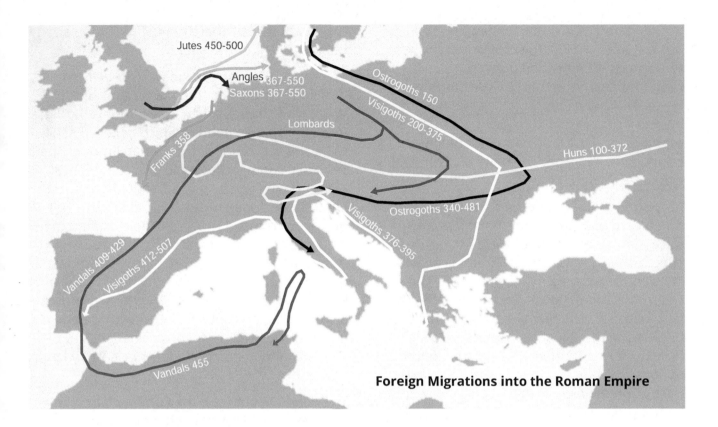

Jutes 450-500

Angles 367-550
Saxons 367-550

Ostrogoths 150

Visigoths 200-375

Lombards

Huns 100-372

Franks 358

Ostrogoths 340-481

Visigoths 376-395

Vandals 409-429

Visigoths 412-507

Vandals 455

Foreign Migrations into the Roman Empire

One city, the City of God, is where the spirit of man lives, and the other is the earthly city where all of the matters of living as a human being occur. Augustine said that all men live in both of these cities all their lives. The City of God is ideal and has all of the rules of God that man must obey. The City of God never disappears like earthly nations, so Christians never have to worry about being without laws of government to protect them.

In the beginning, Augustine said, God gave man dominion over the earth and "... over the fish of the sea, and over the fowl of the air, and over every creeping thing which creepeth on the earth." This dominion, according to Augustine, did not include man having dominion over man. God alone was to rule man. If all men would follow the rules of God, then earthly governments or rulers would have no reason to exist. Because of his concentration on the things of the city of earth, man is enslaved by sin and by other men through rulers and nations.

The best of these earthly governments could only be very bad copies of the City of God, however godly the nation was. Augustine wrote that the basis of nations was sinful, being the domination of one man or men over others. Therefore, to re-create the City of God on earth would be an impossible task. However, Augustine believed that the objective of the true Christian believer must be to continue to try to create on earth as much of the natural order and harmony that existed in the City of God as possible. This objective was to be reached by following the teachings of the church in all things. Among all the impermanent things that existed on earth, one institution would endure throughout time as the best possible reflection of the City of God: the Christian church.

As a reflection of the City of God, the church would always be close to the true natural order of things, the laws of God. Christians would always attempt to make the earthly city more like the City of God by spreading the Word of God. Even though the church might make use of imperfect civil, earthly laws in carrying out the rules of God, this use would only be temporary. Men needed outward rules to remind them of the rule of God that they knew inwardly. After all earthly cities had passed away, all people would follow the natural order of things, and the only nation for man would be the nation of God. The only rules remaining would be the laws of God.

Augustine thought that the best that man could do on earth was to love his neighbor, and in the instances where rules were broken, man should show justice. Justice, treating all persons equally as neighbors, was one of the best reflections of the City of God. Augustine felt that justice should be the basis of all nations because "without justice what else is a kingdom but a huge robbery?" Augustine felt that nations which based their laws on the laws of God, or on the laws of the City of God, were to be obeyed.

The Roman Empire was destroyed by the barbarian invaders and by the rise of separate new nations within the boundaries of the Roman imperial territory. Even as Augustine was dying in AD 430, a new group of invaders were taking the city of Hippo where Augustine had been bishop for thirty-five years.

The thoughts of Augustine were to be the basis of disputes between the new nations of the West, which replaced the rule of Rome, and the Roman Christian church, which believed itself to be the successor of the Roman Empire. The Roman Church, believing itself to be the best reflection of the City of God, thought that it should rule above the kings of the earth. The new kings refused this idea. They justified their power, expansions, creations of new governments, and even their wars on the grounds that they were attempting to model the nations of earth after the City of God. The Roman church also became corrupt as it became more powerful. Its leaders often forsook Christ's call to be servants and instead acted as rich earthly kings and princes.

The disputes between the Roman church and the new governments continued throughout 700 years of war and turmoil after the fall of Rome. This period of history is sometimes called the Dark Ages because of the political chaos. It was the early part of the medieval period.

 Complete this activity.

2.33 Choose one of the places or persons from the following list and write a one-page report. If you choose a place, tell where it is located, mention some of its important rulers or citizens, and classify its governmental system according to the threefold classification of Aristotle. If you choose a person, tell when the person lived, why he was famous, and what sort of government he lived under according to Aristotle's classification system (rule by one, rule by few, rule by many).

Alaric I	Tiberius and Gaius	Marcus Aurelius	Augustus Caesar
Gracchus	Nero	Caligula	Hannibal
Pliny the Elder	Cato	Huns	
Pompeii	Constantine		
Julius Caesar	Vandals		

TEACHER CHECK _____ _____
                                        initials   date

HISTORY & GEOGRAPHY 708

LIFEPAC TEST

NAME _____

DATE _____

SCORE _____

HISTORY & GEOGRAPHY 708: LIFEPAC TEST

Match these items (each answer, 2 points).

1.	_____ Mosaic Code	a.	*City of God*
2.	_____ Thomas Hobbes	b.	knowledge based on logical thought
3.	_____ Plato	c.	laws of the Jews
4.	_____ John Locke	d.	knowledge based on faith
5.	_____ Augustine	e.	*Leviathan*
6.	_____ Machiavelli	f.	the study of who gets what, when, and how
7.	_____ political science	g.	*The Republic*
8.	_____ fideism	h.	*The Prince*
9.	_____ rationalism	i.	*Two Treatises on Civil Government*

Match these items (each answer, 2 points).

10.	_____ explanation and prediction	a.	"render unto Caesar..."
11.	_____ empiricism	b.	the goals of political science
12.	_____ outputs	c.	rule of laws and not men
13.	_____ oligarchy	d.	knowledge based on the senses
14.	_____ John Locke	e.	no laws or government
15.	_____ Augustus	f.	sanctions and symbols
16.	_____ anarchy	g.	Roman emperor at the time of Christ
17.	_____ Aristotle	h.	rule by a few
18.	_____ Luke 20:25	i.	consent of the governed

Complete these statements (each answer, 3 points).

19. According to _____ , the goal of a nation was to gain as much power and prestige as possible.

20. According to _____ , the purpose of the state is to control the evil nature of man and compel him to act morally.

21. Augustine said that the unique event of the a. _____ of
    b. _____ showed that the history of man was not cyclical.

22. Christian political thinkers added to the tradition of Western political thought the ideas of justice and individual _____ .

23. All groups have _____ and leaders.

24. According to _____ , the purpose of the state is to protect the rights of the individual.

Write true or false (each answer, 1 point).

25. _____ Plato said that to correct the evils of government through rational thought was impossible.

26. _____ We cannot be misled by relying on any one of the means of knowledge.

27. _____ Political science is the study of one part of man's culture.

28. _____ Thomas Aquinas believed that the rule of human laws was more important than natural law.

29. _____ Rationalism is accepting facts as knowledge because they fit like the pieces of a puzzle.

Write the letter of the correct answer on the line (each answer, 2 points).

30. The goal of political science is _____ .
    a. description and explanation   b. rational and empirical
    c. not usually stated   d. explanation and prediction

31. The imaginary time before man had laws or governments is called _____ .
    a. the earthly city   b. the City of God   c. the state of nature d. natural law

32. A new tax on real estate is an example of a(n) _____ .
    a. input   b. demand   c. symbol   d. output

33. "The sky is blue" is a(n) _____ .
    a. empirical statement   b. rational statement
    c. silly statement   d. faith statement

34. Epistemology is the study of _____ .
    a. political science   b. how we know what we know
    c. philosophy   d. rationalism

35. "God created the heaven and the earth" is a statement of _____ .
    a. source knowledge   b. empirical knowledge
    c. faith knowledge   d. rational knowledge

Put these people and events in the correct order (each answer, 2 points).

36. _____ Plato

37. _____ Exodus of the Hebrew tribes from Egypt

38. _____ Augustine of Hippo

39. _____ Thomas Hobbes

40. _____ American Revolution

41. _____ Thomas Aquinas

42. _____ The fall of the Roman Empire

Answer this question.

2.34 Which of the following ideas were taught by Augustine of Hippo?
Put a check mark by the correct answers.

_____ History is cyclical.

_____ One event that could never be repeated was the birth of Christ.

_____ The fall of Rome was not vital to Christianity.

_____ The City of God would rise and fall.

_____ The best possible reflection of the City of God was the church.

_____ Man "lives" in two cities–that of God and that of earth.

Write true or false.

2.35 _____ Augustine said that earthly kingdoms rule both man's body and his soul.

2.36 _____ The City of God is where Augustine said the soul of man lives.

2.37 _____ Earthly governments can be good copies of the City of God.

2.38 _____ Augustine said that justice should be the basis of earthly governments.

2.39 _____ Rome was sacked by the Visigoths in AD 410.

2.40 _____ The Roman Empire was destroyed by the barbarians and by the rise of new nations within the empire.

2.41 _____ Augustine felt that men need outward rules to be reminded of how to be good.

Thomas Aquinas. Thomas Aquinas was born in Aquino, Italy, in AD 1225. Little is known of his personal life beyond the fact that he became a member of the Order of the Dominicans in AD 1244 and that he studied and taught at the University of Paris until his death in AD 1274.

The world of Thomas Aquinas was one of turmoil. The nations that were coming into existence at the time of Augustine were now established and were growing in power. During the Dark Ages a series of wars, plagues, and famines had occurred. After about AD 1000 Western civilization began to return to some stability. However, the disputes continued between the church and the new national governments concerning who should be the rulers of man on earth. The thoughts of Thomas Aquinas were directed toward settling this disagreement.

In his most famous book, *Summa Theologica*, Thomas Aquinas gave his views of the government of men. Starting from the assumption of both Aristotle and Augustine that the state exists because men need help to be moral and good, Aquinas concluded that people must consider three types of law when asked by the state to do something. These laws are divine law, natural law, and human law.

Divine law was the Word of God revealed to men. This law was the highest of all possible laws, and man, whatever nation ruled him, was bound to obey the law of God.

The second type of law was *natural law*. Natural law was the feeling inside a person that certain things and actions were either good or bad. Aquinas said that, inwardly, man knows good from evil and that this knowledge had been a part of man from the time he ate of the tree of the knowledge of good and evil in the garden of Eden. All men in the world, whether or not they have had God's divine law revealed to them, know the natural law and can be expected to choose between good and evil.

The third type of law, *human law*, was the rules that kings and nations made for their subjects. These laws were the basis for the community within the state. Human laws told men how to act within a society that was always changing. Therefore, these laws dealt with changeable human things, such as traffic regulations, taxes, fire codes, and all of the other rules that people have to follow in their daily activities.

Thomas Aquinas believed that one of the greatest evils of mankind was that rulers might use human laws to confuse feelings of good and evil. The state would cause men to be confused in their feelings of natural law in order for the state to carry out evil plans. Aquinas was not concerned that man or his government would stray from the divine law because God would safeguard His law. If the human laws of the state came into conflict with natural law, man has no choice but to disobey the ruler. "Therefore if the emperor commands one thing and God another, you must disregard the former and obey God."

Thus, said Aquinas, Augustine was correct in believing that man was enslaved by the state. However, Aquinas concluded that the state only had control over the outward physical being of man. Thomas Aquinas was the first writer who stated that the rule of man over man is only the rule of one physical body over another. Aquinas said that no man rules the soul of another and that the soul is where the true freedom and liberty of man is found. Man's liberty is subject only to the will of God, and no state is powerful enough to take this liberty away.

Four major themes are found in the writings of Thomas Aquinas concerning the relationship of man and his government:

1. Nations exist because men must be able to live together peacefully. Man must have someone to decide earthly conflicts.

2. All men are bound to obey their rulers so that justice and order will exist in human communities. All people will be able to have the benefits and safety of living together.

3. The rule of kings or nations over man are only the rule of man's physical body. A person who has been given orders to violate the inward feelings of natural law need not obey.

4. Whatever earthly government or rules bind man, he is always free in his soul since he has been created equal with all other men before God.

The effects of Christianity and its two greatest political thinkers were important because they added the concepts (ideas) of justice and individual liberty to the tradition of Western political thought.

Augustine taught that no perfect or ideal nations existed because the very idea of nations and rulers was based upon man's enslavement by sin. The best that would happen is that men would try to copy the City of God on earth and in doing so would make justice a part of their kingdoms.

Furthermore, Thomas Aquinas said that men had a dignity of the soul that was beyond the rule of nations. The freedom to know and to choose good over evil, called natural law, was supreme over the laws of the state.

Write true or false.

2.42 _____ Thomas Aquinas based his writings upon the philosophies of Aristotle and Augustine.

Write the letter of the correct answer on the line.

2.43 What were the three types of law Aquinas said must be considered when people were asked by the state to do something? _____
   a. moral, ethical, and physical   b. divine, natural, and human
   c. empirical, rational, and fideism   d. nominal, emotional, and spiritual

2.44 Divine law is the _____ .
   a. knowledge of good and evil   b. Word of God revealed to men
   c. natural form of government   d. part of earthly city

2.45 What was Aquinas afraid that human rulers might use to confuse their subjects about good and evil? _____
   a. mind   b. human laws   c. destiny   d. physical being

2.46 What was the only part of man that can be controlled by the state? _____
   a. mind   b. human laws   c. destiny   d. physical being

2.47 According to Aquinas, man's liberty was subject to the _____ .
   a. laws of the nation   b. rulers of the nation
   c. will of man   d. will of God

Complete these activities.

2.48 Thomas Aquinas' writings contain four main themes concerning the relationship of man and his government. Briefly write the four themes:

a. _____

_____

b. _____

_____

c. _____

_____

d. _____

_____

2.49 Be a philosopher. Thomas Aquinas said that a man need not obey a law that was against the law of God. Read Luke 20:20–26 and Romans 13:1–7. Then decide whether you think that a Christian must obey the laws of a nation. Write your thoughts on a separate sheet of paper and give it to your teacher.

TEACHER CHECK _____ _____

initials   date

Review the material in this section in preparation for the Self Test. This Self Test will check your mastery of this particular section as well as your knowledge of the previous section.

SELF TEST 2

Complete the following crossword (each answer, 2 points).

2.01

ACROSS

1. the Roman emperor at the time of Christ
2. the Roman form of government
3. authored the earliest-known written code of laws
4. barbarians who invaded the Roman Empire
5. wrote *The City of God*
6. wrote *The Politics*
7. said that the sun was the center of the solar system, not the earth
8. the Etruscan king defeated by the Romans

DOWN

1. no laws or government
2. wrote *The Republic*
3. the rule by a few

Complete these statements (each answer, 3 points).

2.02   Most of the philosophers of Augustine's day thought that history was_____ .

2.03   Augustine argued that history was not cyclical because of one unique event—the birth of

_____ .

2.04   Augustine wrote that the a. _____ and fall of nations was only the appearance of

b. _____ things.

2.05   Augustine said that the city of a. _____ is where the spirit of man lives, and the

b. _____ city contains all human concerns.

2.06   The collapse of the Roman Empire was followed by a period called the _____ Ages.

2.07   Aquinas based his writings upon the arguments of a. _____ and

b. _____ .

2.08   Thomas Aquinas wrote that no man has rule over the _____ of another man.

2.09   Christian political thinkers added the concepts of a. _____ and

b. _____ to the tradition of Western political thought.

Match these items (each answer, 2 points).

2.010 _____ empiricism

2.011 _____ rationalism

2.012 _____ fideism

2.013 _____ politics

2.014 _____ epistemology

2.015 _____ public administration

2.016 _____ political science

2.017 _____ Mosaic Code

a.   Old Testament Law

b.   knowledge based on the physical senses

c.   studies, rules, and procedures man uses to govern himself

d.   knowledge based on logical thought

e.   operation of government and public institutions

f.   knowledge based upon faith, feeling, and emotion

g.   the study of how we know what we know

h.   man governing himself

Answer these questions (each numbered answer, 4 points).

2.018 What are the three contributions of Jewish civilization to Western political thought?

a. _____

_____

b. _____

_____

c. _____

_____

2.019 What are the contributions of Greek civilization to Western political thought?

a. _____

_____

b. _____

_____

c. _____

_____

66 / 82   SCORE _____   TEACHER _____ _____
                                        initials   date

3. MODERN POLITICAL SCIENCE

In the second section of this LIFEPAC, you studied how the governments of man changed as his ideas of government changed. The last political thinker you studied, Thomas Aquinas, was a man in a world that was about to experience a revolution in thought.

With the addition of the ideas of Christianity to the political thoughts of the Greeks and the Law of the Jews, a new idea emerged. This idea concerned man as an individual with worth. Each individual person is a human being and, as such, was worthy of being noticed by the state. The new dignity of the individual did not come about because kings had changed their minds or because the new nations of the world granted dignity to man for no reason. This new thought was born out of the ideas of Christianity.

Political thinkers began to wonder: If God recognizes man as an individual and offers him individual salvation through His only Son, then how could the state be more important than the individual?

In this section of the LIFEPAC, you will briefly consider four important modern political thinkers. You will see how two of them, Machiavelli and Hobbes, rejected the new idea of human dignity. You will read how two others, Locke and Mill, accepted this new idea. You will see how some of these men influenced the formation of modern governments. Finally, you will examine a modern system of describing how a government works based upon the ideas of Aristotle.

SECTION OBJECTIVES

Review these objectives. When you have completed this section, you should be able to:

9. List the contributions of some modern political thinkers.

10. Explain the use of models in political science.

11. Construct a model of government based upon current events.

Complete this activity.

3.1 For the next week, read the newspaper and cut out any discussions of politics that appear.

Select several stories about making rules or decisions in government and collect follow-up reports on the following days so that you have at least one complete story. Remember that political science is the study of who gets what, when and how.

Most national and international political news appears in the first two pages of the first section of newspapers while state and local news appears primarily in the first pages of the second and third sections.

Use outside reading materials to learn about the background of the political story or event you are observing. You will use these materials in this section of the LIFEPAC.

TEACHER CHECK _____ _____
initials   date

MODERN POLITICAL THINKERS

The Renaissance, which marks the end of the Dark Ages that Thomas Aquinas knew, also marks the beginning of the period of modern political science. The Renaissance, or Rebirth (approximately 1400–1650 AD), was a period of marvelous achievements in every branch of learning, including political science.

Of the four modern political thinkers you will study, one is an Italian and the other three are Englishmen. The Italian, Machiavelli, and one of the Englishmen, Thomas Hobbes, lived in different time periods. Both of these men, however, lived during times of great social unrest. You will see this unrest reflected in their political thoughts. Both of them believed that the nature of man was evil and that the power of the state was needed to control man's desires.

The other two political thinkers, Locke and Mill, lived during quieter, more stable times. You will see that their thoughts about man and his governments are less gloomy.

Niccolo Machiavelli. Machiavelli was an Italian who lived in the city of Florence between 1469 and 1527 AD He was famous for his reaction to the new notions that men could be more important than the state. Living in a time when rulers assassinated their opponents as a matter of national policy, he suggested that the basis of the state and the ruler's authority is neither justice nor law, but power. Machiavelli wrote in his book, *The Prince*, that the purpose of the nation is to gain as much power and prestige as possible. He also said that any means to this goal can be used and that the ruler of a state was not bound by any ideals of good and evil. No person ruled by the prince had any rights except those that were given by the prince as a bribe for the purpose of keeping order.

Some of Machiavelli's ideas have been used to justify authoritarian states. However, he is important to Western political tradition because he described in detail how the power of the state was used in his time. Machiavelli was the first political scientist to use the empirical method—he described what he saw rather than just stating how he thought things should be.

| Niccolo Machiavelli

Thomas Hobbes. Thomas Hobbes was an Englishman of the seventeenth century (1588-1679) who wrote a book called *Leviathan*. The name *leviathan* is a descriptive word meaning "giant." The giant of which Hobbes was speaking in his book was the modern nation.

Living in a time of great civil war and political unrest in England, Hobbes longed for a more peaceful life and a more stable form of government. Therefore, he described in his book a time in history when he believed that man lived without governments or laws. He called this time in man's history the *state of nature.*

Hobbes was reacting to the continual wars of his age when he wrote that man was constantly warring while in the state of nature. In that state, life, for the most part, was "rude, brutish, and short." Hobbes had little respect for the rational behavior of man living outside of the laws of the state.

From this condition where man was at war with man, the state rose like a leviathan. The purpose of the state was to control the evil nature of man and to compel man to act morally, to cooperate with others, and to act in his own best interests. These things, said Hobbes, could not be expected of man if he were away from the control of the government. The nation that grew from the state of nature would be formed by men because they could no longer live in fear of hunger and death.

Hobbes also wrote that he believed that man had absolute liberty in the state of nature. This liberty allowed man to do whatever he wanted, causing the state of nature to be very cruel. After a time, man was willing to trade all of his liberties to the rulers of a nation in exchange for protection. The only two rights that the person retained under a government were the right of self-defense and the right to demand that the state provide protection against other men.

Complete these statements.

3.2   Machiavelli believed that the basis of the ruler's authority was _____ rather than law or justice.

3.3   Some of Machiavelli's ideas have become the basis for a. _____ states, but he is more important for his use of b. _____ .

3.4   Thomas Hobbes wrote about the modern state, calling it a _____ .

3.5   The imaginary time in history when man lived without laws or government was called the _____ .

3.6   Hobbes believed that the state existed to control the _____ of man.

Answer these questions.

3.7   What kind of liberty did Hobbes believe man had in the state of nature? _____

3.8   What liberties or rights did Hobbes say man had under the rule of a government?

   a. _____

   b. _____

3.9   According to Machiavelli, what were the purposes of the state?

   a. _____   b. _____

John Locke. The Englishman John Locke (1632-1704) wrote a book called *Two Treatises on Civil Government* in which he discussed the same state of nature of which Hobbes wrote. Unlike Hobbes, who believed in the absolute authority of the state, Locke believed in the rights of man. He believed that in the state of nature, man lived according to natural law and had a life that was peaceful and full of reason. Locke said that man might have remained in this ideal state except that man must have the help and cooperation of other men. The conditions in the state of nature, when each person was allowed to do whatever he wanted, did not allow certain activities, such as building roads or schools. Therefore, men banded together and formed nations to accomplish the things which they could not do separately.

In the state of nature, according to Locke, man obeyed natural law. A man had rights and freedom equal with those of every other man because God had created all men equal. Because the rights or dignities of man had existed before the nations were formed, and because man formed the nations to serve him, no state could take away the rights of its citizens.

John Locke said that natural law and natural rights were the limits of the government's power. If the rulers of a nation acted as tyrants or dictators, then, according to Locke, they "have put themselves into a state of war with the people who are absolved from any further obedience...." If this state occurred, the people had a right to establish a new form of government which would provide for the safety and security of the people.

Locke's basic ideas are that no government can exist without the consent of the governed and that the primary purpose of the state was to protect the rights of the citizen.

John Stuart Mill. *The Essay on Liberty*, by John Stuart Mill, is one of the most important political science books ever written. By the time this book was written (1869) the United States had already become a nation and had fought a Civil War over the rights of men. Living in England, Mill observed the conditions in the United States and elsewhere and decided that the new ideas of the rights of man could be carried too far. He reasoned that the problem of freedom in a democracy is not how the nation or ruler treats the people, but how the majority of the people treat the minority. Mill reminds us that the rights that men have, such as participating in making the rules of a nation, are not absolute. The freedom of any man is limited by the freedom his neighbor enjoys.

John Stuart Mill said that the purpose of the state is not only to protect the rights of the individual but, more importantly, to protect the rights of minorities from the power of the majority in a democracy.

 Write the letter of the correct answer on the line.

3.10 Unlike Hobbes, who believed in the authority of the state, John Locke believed in _____ .
    a. divine rights
    b. authoritarianism
    c. the rights of man
    d. the cruelty of the state of nature

3.11 John Locke stressed that the limits of government power were natural rights and _____ .
    a. the state of nature
    b. natural law
    c. divine law
    d. rational thought

3.12 Locke said that no government could exist without the consent of _____ .
    a. the governed
    b. a constitution of laws
    c. the king
    d. the prince

3.13 John Stuart Mill decided that the rights of man should be _____ .
    a. absolute
    b. self-evident
    c. found in the state of nature
    d. limited

3.14 Locke said that the primary purpose of government was the _____ of rights.
    a. protection
    b. return
    c. granting
    d. denial

POLITICAL THEORY AND PRACTICE

In the governments of the Western world today, many examples exist showing how the political thoughts that you have studied are put into practice. The Declaration of Independence and the Constitution of the United States best show how the tradition of Western political thought was put into practice. Constitutions throughout the world, including many in authoritarian governments, use the political thoughts that are expressed in the Constitution and Declaration of Independence. (Because of the length of the United States Constitution, you will concentrate on the Declaration of Independence. However, for extra learning experience, you should use the encyclopedia and read the Constitution. Attempt to determine the origin of some of the political ideas.)

Thomas Jefferson had studied political science and had read Locke's *Two Treatises on Civil Government* while he was in college. He was very impressed with the ideas of John Locke, especially with the idea that no government could exist without the approval of the people. Jefferson also believed that if a government treated its citizens unfairly, the citizens could break away and form a new government.

In the summer of 1776, Thomas Jefferson wrote the Declaration of Independence. He used many of the ideas and even some of the exact words of John Locke in this work. This Declaration was the foundation of the new nation that was to be called the United States of America.

The ideas of Locke were very influential because the frontier of the American colonies must have seemed very much like the state of nature that Western political thinking had described. Some of the early colonists, such as the Pilgrims in 1620, made compacts or contracts with each other. These compacts were much like those in the state of nature described by both Locke and Hobbes. The Declaration of Independence is a compact between the people of the colonies. People believed that they were living without government, almost in a state of nature.

| Thomas Jefferson

The Declaration of Independence has two main parts. The first two paragraphs are called the preamble and contain most of the political thoughts that you have studied in this LIFEPAC. The remainder, or body, of the Declaration lists the specific actions of King George that the colonists thought were wrong.

The preamble of the Declaration of Independence is called the Bill of Rights, and it contains five main thoughts. Each of these thoughts is part of the tradition of Western political thought:

1. God has granted equality to all men;

2. All men have equal rights at birth,

3. The basic human rights are life, liberty, and the pursuit of happiness,

4. The rights of humans are *self-evident*, or obvious, to any person using rational thought; and

5. If a government takes away human rights, the people may abolish (do away with) the government.

Complete this activity.

3.15 Read the first two paragraphs of the Declaration of Independence. On a separate piece of paper, copy each phrase that you think is part of the tradition of Western political thought. You have already seen most of the ideas you will read in the previous sections of this LIFEPAC. Compare your findings with those of a classmate.

HELPER CHECK _____ _____
                                       initials   date.

Complete these statements.

3.16 In the summer of 1776, _____ wrote the Declaration of Independence.

3.17 The frontier of the American colonies must have seemed like the state of nature that

a. _____ and b. _____ had described.

3.18 The body of the Declaration of Independence lists actions of King a. _____ which the colonists thought were b. _____ .

3.19 The a. _____ were early American colonists who made b. _____ or contracts with each other.

A MODEL OF GOVERNMENT

Many forms of government exist today, and many others have passed out of existence. As you have seen in your study of political thought, the ways in which men form and view their governments depend much on the conditions and events of the times.

The Hebrews based their government almost exclusively on fideism and followed a single leader who was selected by God. The Greeks established the concept of the nation which could be created, directed, and served by rational thought. Christian thought added the ideas of the Greeks and the Hebrews together and, with ideas special to Christianity, created the idea of the state as the servant of man.

Although modern political scientists still debate the basis of the leader's powers and the rights of the individual, they are more concerned with the description of events within the nation.

Because so many forms of government occur in the world, made up of so many different peoples, the differences among these governments would be impossible to study. To solve this problem, political scientists look at the similarities among governments. They study the inputs and outputs of government and form models to determine the best possible form of government.

| Decision-making box

Political environment. You have seen that all groups of people have leaders and have rules based on the religious and philosophical views of the majority of the group. In the language of twentieth-century political scientists, these views comprise the *political environment*.

Each person on earth is raised within several environments. These include a social environment, such as being American, British, Chinese, or Eskimo; a physical environment, the place and climate where you live; and a political environment, what you and the people around you believe about politics. Persons born into a certain culture usually take on the beliefs, knowledge, and correct ways of behavior of that culture.

The political environment is where beliefs about rule-making and politics are found. For the most part, government is a reflection of the beliefs of the majority of the people in a nation. Because we have a two-party system, two houses of Congress, and base our laws on a Constitution, our government is as much a reflection of our political environment as the government of the Athenian city-state was of the Greek political environment.

The workings of any government can be described through a close examination of the political environment. Imagine that the place where decisions are made (the government) is

a small box within the political government: the congress, the president, the courts, and other rule-making bodies.

According to Aristotle, only three forms of government can be found in this "decision-making box": rule of one, rule of a few, and rule of many.

Look at the *rule of one illustration*. The arrows show which way the communication flows most of the time between rulers and those they rule. One person is absolute ruler over all things, and all his decisions go out through the people he has appointed. Notice that decisions originate only at the top and that only minor decisions are made by the appointed officials. This model is one of authoritarian government.

Look at the *rule of a few* illustration. an oligarchy. Like the *rule of one,* rules are made at the top. However, the people in charge of the *rule of a few* are more or less equal and must consult each other before decisions are made.

The last form of government is the *rule of many*. Although varying in practice, *the rule of many* can be diagrammed like the illustration.

The decisions on major issues are made by all citizens. If the population of a nation is too large for all of the citizens to participate directly in government, the people elect representatives to look after the interests of the government.

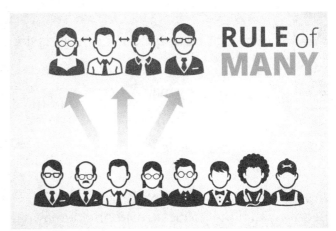

To make decisions, leaders must be presented with problems to solve and must have information upon which to solve the problems.

This information comes from the same place as the rulers and political beliefs—the political environment.

 Complete these activities.

3.20 List three types of environments in which people live.

a. _____ b. _____

c. _____

3.21 The concept of the nation that could be created, directed, and served by rational thought was established by the _____ .

3.22 Government is a reflection of the beliefs of the _____ of the people in a nation.

3.23 Explain the differences among Aristotle's three classifications of government.

a. _____

_____

b. _____

_____

c. _____

_____

Match each description of how decisions are made with Aristotle's classifications of government.

3.24 _____ rule by many

3.25 _____ rule by one

3.26 _____ rule by few

a. made at the top

b. consultation among rulers

c. citizens have direct participation

Inputs and outputs. People or groups of people within the political environment may ask the government to start doing something about a particular problem or to continue a course of action. These requests from the people in the political environment are called _inputs_. Two types of inputs occur: _support_s and _demands._

Demands are inputs into the decision-making box that ask the decision makers to do something. A letter to a congressman is a demand similar to a petition of a king. Voting can be a _demand_ if it is for the opposition party. It can also be a _support_ if it is for the party in power.

Supports are inputs from the citizens that tell the decision makers in the government they are doing a good job. _Supports_ can be votes, the payment of taxes, or even cheering when the leader of a group or nation rides in a parade.

Decisions are also made on the other side of the decision box. Those decisions that come from, and are enforced by, the government are called _outputs_. Outputs may cause much turmoil in the political environment because, although some people may be happy with a decision, others will be unhappy. In this case new demands will be made upon the government. Three types of outputs from the decision box occur: _rewards, sanctions,_ and _symbols._

Rewards are demands that have been agreed to by the government. If a group asks for a law to make cars safer, to build a dam, or to cut taxes, and that law is passed, then this action is a _reward. Sanctions_ are punishments. The government may refuse the demands of a person

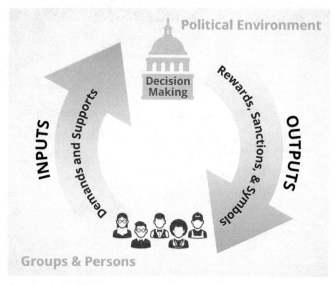

| Decision box

or group, or a new rule which was demanded may penalize a certain group of citizens. For instance, the town government's refusal to install a new crosswalk and new laws which make driving over fifty-five miles per hour illegal are sanctions.

Symbols are actions by the government that are designed to keep the citizens happy and aware that the rulers are paying attention to them. A parade with the army band playing patriotic tunes and local representatives making speeches are symbols. Other symbols are the government awarding prizes, medals, or honors to persons or groups.

A unique characteristic of an output is its variable application. One person will consider a government decision a reward, someone else will consider the same action a sanction, and another person will consider it a symbol.

Answer this question.

3.27 What is the difference between a support and a demand? _____

_____

_____

_____

Write *I* for input or *O* for output on the line.

3.28 _____ a letter to a congressman

3.29 _____ a picket line of union members demanding new rules

3.30 _____ a Veterans Day parade

3.31 _____ voting

3.32 _____ a tax increase

3.33 _____ a new super highway

3.34 _____ a law against frisbees

3.35 _____ a parent-teacher resolution to ask the state for new books

Models. Diagramming and drawing pictures of government decision making is called modeling and is done quite often by political scientists. Making models of government is very much like making wood or plastic models of airplanes or ships. The only difference between these models, other than the subject matter, is that the models of government have many more pieces. Some models of politics or governments may contain many thousands of inputs and outputs. Instead of the glue usually used in constructing the models you are used to, the political models may require the use of a computer to count, order, and put together all of the pieces. The finished political science model should be able to explain what is happening in the political environment and, hopefully, to predict what is likely to occur in the future.

As an example of modeling and its subject matter, consider this problem:

A river in a congressional district in the north floods each year and damages the crops of some of the farmers who live along the river. The farmers in the area organized a group called Stop the Waters, or STW. This organization collected money from the farmers and sent one of the members of STW to Congress to ask for funds to build a dam. When this demand was made public, a group of hunters and fishermen, afraid that the new dam would harm hunting and fishing, organized a group called Keep It Flowing (KIF). This group petitioned Congress not to build the dam. They also had editors of newspapers friendly to their views write articles praising the government for keeping the area around the proposed dam a wilderness area. The Congress sent out representatives to speak to the local groups and promised that some action would be taken.

After a long debate, the decision was made to build a dam. At this time the farmers organized a community picnic with bands, parades, and speeches by local and national leaders.

The hunters and fishermen quietly gathered their forces and collected funds for an attempt to demand that the decision on the dam be changed.

The demands and supports over the issue of the dam both started with some event in the environment. Both groups made demands upon the government, and one group, KIF, used newspapers to show support for the government.

The reward for STW was a new dam and all the symbols of flags, parades, and speeches. At the same time, the KIF forces had received a sanction, which they were using as the basis of a new demand. Until the dam is built, and perhaps long afterwards, the cycle of inputs (demands and supports) and outputs (rewards, sanctions, and symbols) will continue.

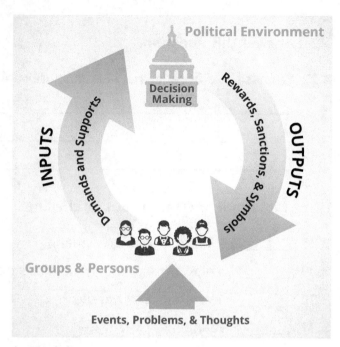

| Modeling

The political process of all governments follow this cycle:

1. An event, problem, or thought occurs in the environment.

2. Citizens react to that event, problem, or thought.

3. Citizens form inputs to the government through demands or supports.

4. Government responds to the citizens through outputs of rewards, sanctions, and symbols.

5. Outputs form the basis for further inputs.

Complete this activity.

3.36 Construct a model government to solve the political issue you have studied. The articles on political events you have collected from the newspapers will be used to show how the process of politics works.

First, identify each group or leader of each group, and write a short paragraph stating how each group perceives the issue.

Second, label the inputs of each group as being either a demand or a support. Both groups could be making demands if no government plans pertaining to the issue presently exist.

Third, label all the outputs according to whether they are rewards, sanctions, or symbols. If the issue has not yet been settled, use your imagination and attempt to predict what might happen.

Draw your model government on paper using different colors, and include your explanation of what is happening and what the outcome might be.

TEACHER CHECK _____ _____
                       initials   date

Before you take this last Self Test, you may want to do one or more of these self checks.

1. _____ Read the objectives. See if you can do them.
2. _____ Restudy the material related to any objectives that you cannot do.
3. _____ Use the **SQ3R** study procedure to review the material:
   a. **S**can the sections.
   b. **Q**uestion yourself.
   c. **R**ead to answer your questions.
   d. **R**ecite the answers to yourself.
   e. **R**eview areas you did not understand.
4. _____ Review all vocabulary, activities, and Self Tests, writing a correct answer for every wrong answer.

SELF TEST 3

Match these items (each answer, 2 points).

3.01	_____ political theory	a.	consent of the governed
3.02	_____ Hobbes	b.	the study of the history of thoughts about government
3.03	_____ politics		
3.04	_____ John Locke	c.	rights of the minority
3.05	_____ Machiavelli	d.	*Leviathan*
3.06	_____ fideism	e.	Mosaic Code
3.07	_____ political science	f.	the process of man's governing himself
3.08	_____ outputs	g.	rules of laws and not men
3.09	_____ John Locke	h.	*Two Treatises on Civil Government*
3.010	_____ Aristotle	i.	sanctions and symbols
3.011	_____ the Jews	j.	*The Prince*
3.012	_____ John Stuart Mill	k.	knowledge based on faith
		l.	explanation and prediction

Put these people, events, and places in the proper order, from oldest (1) to newest (8) (each answer, 2 points).

3.013 _____ Aristotle

3.014 _____ Augustus Caesar

3.015 _____ Thomas Hobbes

3.016 _____ Exodus of the Hebrew tribes from Egypt

3.017 _____ Plato

3.018 _____ American Revolution

3.019 _____ Augustine of Hippo

3.020 _____ Greek city-states

Match the names of these individuals with their philosophies (each answer, 2 points).

3.021 _____ Machiavelli

3.022 _____ Thomas Hobbes

3.023 _____ John Locke

3.024 _____ John Stuart Mill

3.025 _____ Plato

3.026 _____ Aristotle

3.027 _____ Thomas Aquinas

3.028 _____ Augustine

a. man is always free in his soul

b. the state should gain as much power and prestige as possible

c. three kinds of government; rule by one; rule by few; rule by many

d. the nation exists to control the evil nature of man

e. government came from the mind of man

f. the primary purpose of government is to protect the rights of citizens

g. the freedom of a man is limited by his neighbor's freedom

h. history is a line of man's development that includes the City of God and earthly cities

Write the letter of the correct answer on the line (each answer, 2 points).

3.029 The rule of a few is a(n) _____ .
a. authoritarian government
c. state
b. oligarchy
d. hierarchy

3.030 A new tax on property is an example of a(n) _____ .
a. input
b. demand
c. symbol
d. output

3.031 A letter from the governor of your state congratulating your class on its high marks in political science is a(n) _____ .
a. input
b. support
c. symbol
d. joke

Write true or false (each answer, 1 point).

3.032 _____ Political science is the oldest of the social sciences.

3.033 _____ Political science is the study of who gets what, when and how.

3.034 _____ "He has blue eyes" is a statement based on rational knowledge.

3.035 _____ An authoritarian government is ruled by one person.

3.036 _____ The Greeks formed small kingdoms called city-states.

3.037 _____ Augustine believed that the Roman Empire must survive.

3.038 _____ All groups have both leaders and rules.

3.039 _____ Political science is the study of the laws, leaders, and people who make up a nation.

3.040 _____ The *Torah* was the Old Testament law books.

3.041 _____ The Greeks created the political system called a republic.

3.042 _____ "The Lord is my shepherd" is a statement based on faith.

Complete these statements (each answer, 3 points).

3.043 Knowledge based on the senses is called _____ knowledge.

3.044 A person who may ask questions about how governments are formed is called a political

_____ .

3.045 The study of how we know what we know is called _____ .

3.046 Rational knowledge is based on _____ thought.

Complete the list (each answer, 3 points).

3.047 List three contributions of Jewish civilization to Western political thought.

a. _____

b. _____

c. _____

74 / 93   SCORE _____   TEACHER _____ _____

Before taking the LIFEPAC Test, you may want to do one or more of these self checks.

1. _____ Read the objectives. See if you can do them.
2. _____ Restudy the material related to any objectives that you cannot do.
3. _____ Use the SQ3R study procedure to review the material.
4. _____ Review activities, Self Tests, and LIFEPAC vocabulary words.
5. _____ Restudy areas of weakness indicated by the last Self Test.